For Moses Renee and Curtis Flood—B.P.

To my parents—J.A.

No part of this publication may be reproduced in whole or in part, or stored in a retrieval system,
or transmitted in any form or by any means, electronic, mechanical, photocopying, recording,
or otherwise, without written permission of the publisher. For information regarding permission,
write to NorthSouth Books, 600 Third Avenue, 2nd Floor, New York, NY 10016.

Text copyright © 2018 by Baptiste Paul.
Illustrations copyright © 2018 by Jacqueline Alcántara.
All rights reserved. Published by Scholastic Inc., 557 Broadway, New York, NY 10012,
by arrangement with NorthSouth Books.
Printed in the U.S.A.

ISBN-13: 978-1-338-65303-8
ISBN-10: 1-338-65303-2

SCHOLASTIC and associated logos are trademarks
and/or registered trademarks of Scholastic Inc.

7 8 9 10   40   28 27 26 25 24 23 22 21

Scholastic Inc., 557 Broadway, New York, NY 10012

THE FIELD

words by **Baptiste Paul** · pictures by **Jacqueline Alcántara**

SCHOLASTIC INC.

Vini! Come!

The field calls.

2

Bol. Ball.

Soulye. Shoes.

Goal. Goal.

Ou. Ou. Ou. You. You. You.
Friends versus friends.

Annou ale! Let's go!

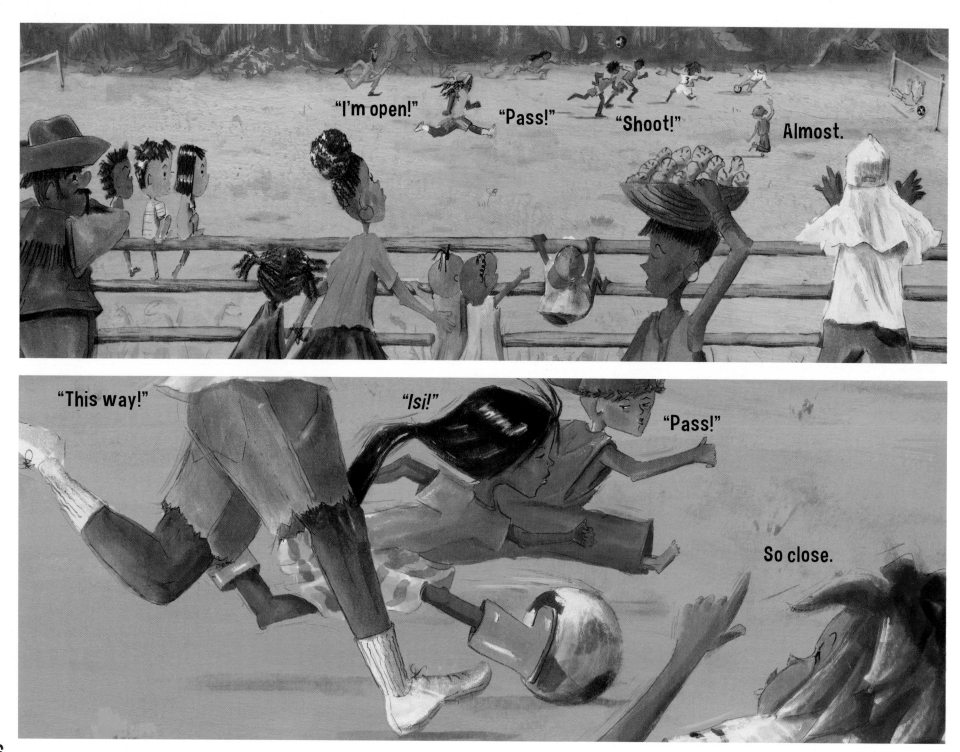

6

Uh-oh.

Shutters bang.
Sun hides.
Clay dust stings.
Sky falls.

Fini? Game over?

"Play on!"

Dash.

Splash.

"Time-out!"

Shoes off.
Socks off.
GO!

Run.
Side to side.
Kick.
Jump.

"Oops!"

Ou byen? You okay?
Mwen byen. I'm good.

13

Rain stops.
Sun peeks.

14

One last drive.
Dribble, twist...

GOOOOOOOOOOOOOOOOOAL!

High fives.
Fist-bumps.
Happy tackles.

Mamas call.
Vini! Come!

We play on.

Vini, abwezan! Come now!

Game pauses.

Mamas press their lips.

Soaked shoes.
Dirty shirts.
Mud-caked kids.
Torn-up field.

We hide our smiles.
We slip into the tub.

22

We dream about *futbol*.
We dream about friends.
Until the field calls again.

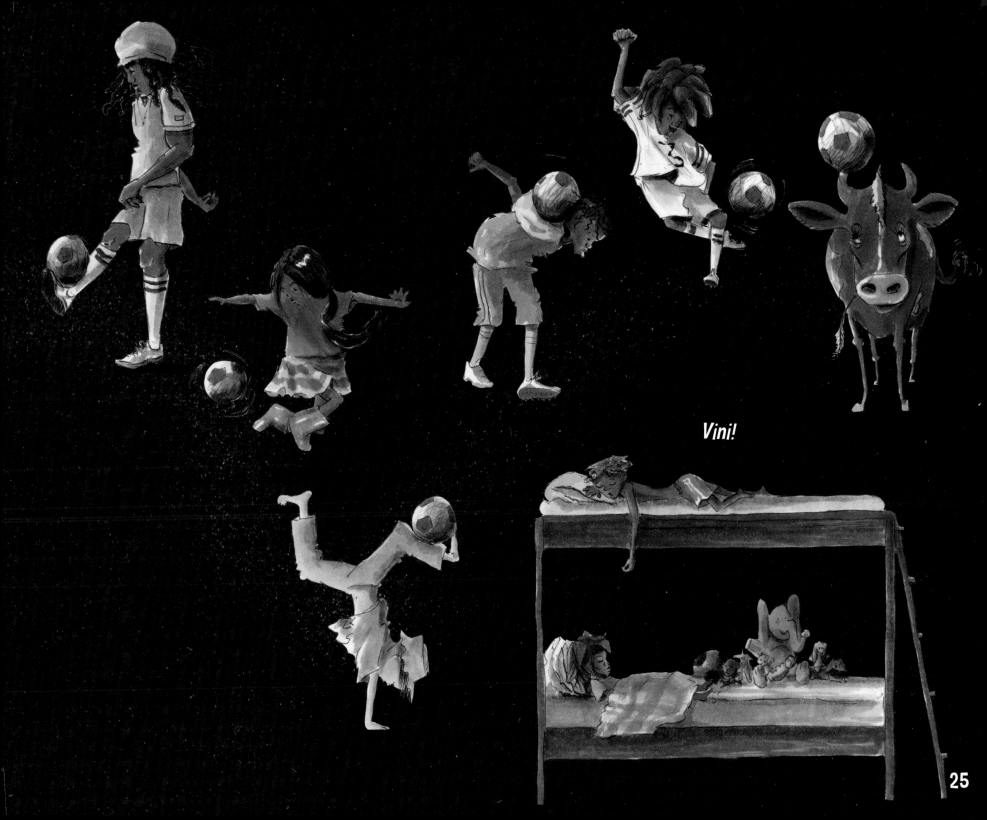

Vini!

Author's Note

As a kid growing up, I did not have electricity, running water, or many toys. What I did have plenty of were siblings—nine of them—and lots of friends. Most of my free time was spent on a *futbol* (soccer) field playing, learning new techniques, and occasionally getting bruised. When I see my children run outside to play, it reminds me of my childhood.

In *The Field*, children overcome many barriers that threaten to end their game. In life, things rarely happen as we plan, but the way we keep playing through challenges makes us who we are. Today, I still get the chills watching a soccer game. I go crazy or, what my son would say, "coo coo nuts" when my team scores a GOOOOOOOAAALLLL! I love the concept of play: everyone cheering together, forgetting about whatever challenges life can bring.

Creole is a language spoken by peoples of several Caribbean islands, including Haiti, Saint Lucia, and Dominica. In *The Field*, you'll notice that some of the Saint Lucian Creole words are similar to French, English, Hindi, and other languages—because many people who live on the island either speak or have ancestors who spoke these languages.

Even more amazing is that since people rarely write in Creole (they mostly speak it), new words are always being added and older words tend to change or get forgotten. This is one reason each island's "Creole" sounds a little different.

Bibliography (for Saint Lucian Creole spellings/accent marks)
Crosbie, Paul, et al. *Kwéyòl Dictionary*. Edited by David Frank, 1st ed., Castries, Saint Lucia, Ministry of Education, Government of Saint Lucia, 2001, www.saintluciancreole.dbfrank.net/dictionary/KweyolDictionary.pdf. Accessed 31 Jan. 2016.

Creole Words and Phrases

Creole words	English
abwezan (ah-BWAY-zah)	right now
Annou alé (An-OO-ah-LAY)	Let's go
bol (BOWL)	ball
Bonswè (bone-SWAA)	Good night
fini (FEE-nee)	done/finished
futbol (FUT-boll)	soccer
isi (EE-see)	here
Mwen (MWAY)	I
Mwen byen (MWAY bee-EH)	I'm good
Ou byen (OO-bee-EH)	Are you okay?
Ou ou ou (OO, oo, oo)	You, you, you!
Shoo (SHOO)	Move! Go away
soulye (SOOL-yee-ay)	shoes
Vini (VEE-nee)	Come
Vini abwézan (VEE-nee ah-BWAY-zah)	Come right now